Arctic Ocean
Iqaluit
Atlantic Ocean
NEWFOUNDLAND
Labrador
QUEBEC
Parson's Pond
St. John's
Witless Bay
ONTARIO
Gaspé Peninsula
Chicoutimi
Charlottetown
PRINCE EDWARD ISLAND
Kapuskasing
Thunder Bay
Quebec City
St. John
Halifax
NOVA SCOTIA
Lake Superior
Lake Nippissing
Cornwall
St. Lawrence
Ottawa
NEW BRUNSWICK
Toronto
Niagara Falls

See Saw Saskatchewan

More Playful Poems from Coast to Coast

Written by Robert Heidbreder

Illustrated by Scot Ritchie

Kids Can Press

To Jane, my partner in Canada —R. H.

To the memory of my dad, who liked the wide open spaces —S.R.

Kids Can Press acknowledges the financial support of the Ontario Arts Council, the Canada Council for the Arts and the Government of Canada, through the BPIDP, for our publishing activity.

Kids Can Press Ltd.
29 Birch Avenue
Toronto, ON M4V 1E2

www.kidscanpress.com

Edited by Tara Walker
Designed by Julia Naimska
Printed and bound in Hong Kong, China, by Book Art Inc., Toronto

The hardcover edition of this book is smyth sewn casebound.

CM 03 0 9 8 7 6 5 4 3 2 1

National Library of Canada Cataloguing in Publication Data

Heidbreder, Robert
See saw Saskatchewan : more playful poems from coast to coast / written by Robert Heidbreder ; illustrated by Scot Ritchie.

Includes index.

ISBN 1-55337-392-8

1. Canada — Juvenile poetry. 2. Children's poetry, Canadian (English) 3. Rhyming Games — Juvenile literature. I. Ritchie, Scot II. Title.

PS8565.E42S42 2003 jC811'.54 C2002-903143-5
PZ7

Kids Can Press is a Corus™ Entertainment company

On Your Mark …

Get ready for more read-along, rhyme-along fun! *See Saw Saskatchewan* is full of playful poems and kooky characters that will make you want to kick up your heels and join in their fun. Sing a tune with an Ontario loon, plunge into a prairie wheat pool, pick a peck of P.E.I., and cancan your way across Canada!

You'll find poems you can bounce balls to. Others make great skipping rhymes. Some are perfect for doing actions, others for playing clapping games with a partner. And when it's time to pick teams or decide who's "It," just choose a choosing rhyme. Many of the rhymes in *See Saw Saskatchewan* have a symbol or two like the ones below to get you started.

But the symbols don't mean there's only one way to play with these poems. Try making up your own games. Add some actions to a skipping rhyme. Make up a silly dance for another. Think of a funny way to chant your favourite poem with some friends. No matter how you like to play, the poems in *See Saw Saskatchewan* can add to your fun. So go ahead: turn the page, read a rhyme and start playing!

Skate Canada

See saw Saskatchewan,
bumping up and down.
Swing Manitoba
high off the ground.
Hide-and-seek Ontario,
peeking in and out.
Skateboard New Brunswick,
whizzing all about.
Hopscotch Newfoundland
and Labrador's shores.
Parachute Alberta
through the wide outdoors.
Slide around Quebec —
whee! what fun!
Water raft B.C.
on every river run.

Sprint the Northwest Territories —
time how fast you race!
Hang-glide Nunavut,
peering down from space.
Trampoline P.E.I.,
flying through the sky.
Rock climb bright Yukon,
scaling up so high.
Sail Nova Scotia
as the sea winds blow.
Then …
hockey-skate all Canada
when winter brings the snow.
Across the silver ice
grab a stick and go
go
GO!

Rocky Mountain Mountain Goats

Rocky Mountain mountain goats
race along steep peaks.
Rocky Mountain mountain goats
play mountain hide-and-seek.
Rocky Mountain mountain goats
play mountain goat leapfrog.
Rocky Mountain mountain goats
dance in mountain clogs.
Rocky Mountain mountain goats
bend their hairy knees,
then Rocky Mountain mountain goats
dive into Lake Louise!

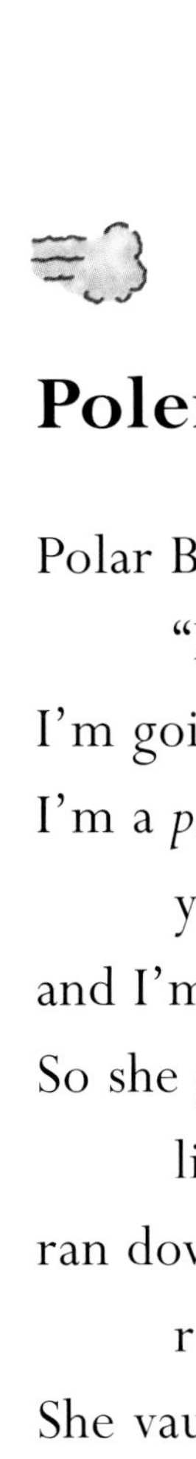

Poler Polar Bear

Polar Bear griped:
    "I hate fishing!
I'm going to do what I've been wishing.
I'm a *polar* bear,
    you see,
and I'm going to be the POLAR ME!"
So she grabbed a pole,
    limber and strong,
ran down the ice,
    rushing headlong.
She vaulted over a wide ice floe,
    a tall iceberg
    and a bank of snow.
She somersaulted on the other side,
sprung herself up and smiled with pride:
    "Now I'm a BEAR
    and a POLER, too.
    I'm a polar bear
    through and through."

Boss Ross Albatross

Boss Ross Albatross
played lacrosse
with a ball of moss,
filled the field
with applesauce
and strung his stick
with dental floss.
"I always floss when I play lacrosse,"
beamed Boss Ross Albatross.

Eager Beaver Antoinette

Eager Beaver Antoinette
logged onto the Internet,
worked all night,
built a site,
computer crashed
like dynamite —
SLAM!
BAM!
WHOOEY!
WHAM!
"Next time,"
she said,
"I'll build a … DAM!"

Did you know that "chesterfield" is the Canadian word for "sofa"?

Hester Jester Chesterfield

Hester Jester Chesterfield
dug some rows
and hoed and heeled,
sprinkled stuffing,
bits of springs,
covers, pillows,
twines and strings.
"In spring,"
she winked,
"this field yields
the finest crop
of chesterfields!"

Jake Jake Garter Snake

Jake Jake Garter Snake
rolled himself
into Reindeer Lake,
sprang back out
with a slippery shake
and said to Reindeer,
"MY MISTAKE!"
O – U – T
Out goes Jake!

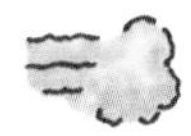

Fool's Gold

We tumbled down
in Tumbler Ridge,
just like Jack and Jill,
and when our tumbling
was all done,
we were in Barkerville.
There we found a stream
with gold,
enough to fill Gaspé,
and by the way,
I guess you know …
it's APRIL FOOL'S DAY!

One Nanaimo Bar

For fiddleheads a penny,
For bannock a dime,
A nickel for some tourtière,
A quarter for perogy time.
A loonie for some maple pie,
A toonie for a sugar star —
But all the GST you want
For one Nanaimo bar!

Try spinning faster and faster as you say this rhyme. Then fall down on the last line!

The King's Underpants

The King,
he left old London.
He travelled to New France
and danced the hokey-pokey
in his royal underpants.
His underpants flew off
as he shook his royal bum.
He shouted:
"Back to New France
never will I come!"

A Musical Ride

Little Monty Mountie
took a drum,
a tuba,
some cymbals,
a banjo to strum,
hopped on his horse
and proudly cried:
"I'm ready to go
on a musical ride!"

Snowbirds

Raven was a-ravin'
about the ice and snow.
"Quit your complainin',"
cawed old friend Crow.
"If you're cravin' sunshine,
if you're cravin' heat,
Florida's a haven
you sure can't beat!
So quit ravin'
Raven,
and fly with me —
Wing it south
to sun, fun and sea!"

The common raven is the official bird of the Yukon Territory.

Friends

U.S.A. south,
Canada north,
cross the border,
back and forth.
Canada loonie,
U.S.A. buck,
paddle a canoe,
then drive a truck.
U.S.A. eagle,
and Canada goose,
Okanagan apples,
Florida orange juice.
U.S.A. starts
where Canada ends,
U.S.A.,
Canada,
shake hands, friends!

The Seas We Share

Won't you see the sea I see?
Come and see the sea by me.

See the sea that I can see,
the Atlantic rolling free.

Won't you hear the sea I hear?
Pounding sounding loud and clear.

Hear the sea that I can hear,
the Pacific crashing near.

Won't you feel the sea I feel?
Freezing foaming at my heel.

Feel the sea that I can feel,
icy Arctic cold as steel.

Won't you smell the sea I smell?
Warm and golden earth seashell.

Smell the sea that I can smell,
waving grain in summer's spell.

And won't you taste the sea I taste?
The sea of wind around my face.

Taste and feel the sea of air,
smell, see, hear the seas we share.

Niagara Falls

Kapuskasing sings,
Cornwall calls,
Thunder Bay storms,
And Niagara
FALLS!

Waterways

Sail Lake Superior.
Blow, wind, blow.

Raft down the Yukon.
Whitewater, go!

Row down the Bow.
So merrily afloat.

Skim Lake Nipissing.
Vrooom! motorboat.

Barge the Mackenzie.
Push and lug.

Tug the St. Lawrence.
Chug! Chug! Chug!

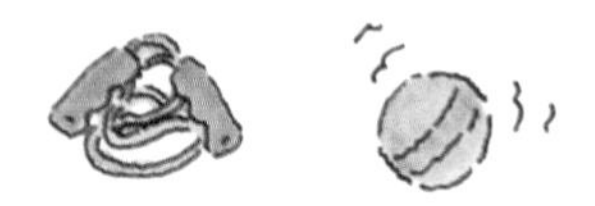

Ready Eddie Edmonton

Ready Eddie Edmonton
ran a barenaked prairie run,
burned his bum in the noonday sun,
covered it with hot cross buns.
"Buns on the buns make running fun!"
said Ready Eddie Edmonton.

How many buns did he wear on his run?

"Paree" Marie

"Paree" Marie
from Chicoutimi
stirred maple sugar in her tea,
climbed the best tree she could see,
then sat at the top to dine on brie.

How many trees did "Paree" Marie see?
1, 2, 3 — you're with me!

These poems end with a challenge. How many times can you jump before you trip?

Muddled Millie New Brunswick

Muddled Millie New Brunswick
got lost in P.E.I.,
on a winter's day
in the middle of July!
The sun was shining
bright that night.
The cats were all out barking.
The dogs were caterwauling
and the butterflies were larking.
The sun was setting in the east.
The north was to the west.
And the cows up in the trees
were building a crow's nest.
The sea was dry with April dew …
and Muddled Millie New Brunswick
declared that she was you!

Pick a Peck of P.E.I.

Pick a peck of P.E.I.,
pack it in a box.
Send it off to Newfoundland,
get back a box of ...
rocks!

Stuff the rocks
in dirty socks,
then haul them to the shore.
Swing 'em fling 'em
in the sea,
then start again once more ...

This is called a circular poem because it keeps going around and around and around ...

Take Toronto by the Toe

Take Toronto by the toe.
Grab it,
    Nab it,
Don't let go!
    Clip its toenails.
    Comb its hair.
    Put it in fresh underwear.
Clean its ears.
Wash its feet.
Then walk it up and down
    Yonge Street!

Silly-Billy Lily

Silly-Billy Lily
pulled a western red lily
and took it willy-nilly
to chilly Picadilly,
where she gave it to the Queen
tied up with a sardine.
"Oh, nothing's truly finer
than red lilies from Regina
for the finest of Reginas
that I've surely ever seen!"
said Silly-Billy Lily
as she curtsied to the Queen.

The western red lily is the provincial flower of Saskatchewan.

Alberta Rose

Alberta Rose
rose up with the sun
and off she dozed
when day was done.
She dozed all night in a flowerbed
with roses from her feet to head.
"I know it's wild," Alberta said,
"but roses are the best bedspread
from A B C to X Y ZED."

The wild rose is the provincial flower of Alberta.

How fast can you say these tongue-twisters?

Dogwood's Bark

How many barks
would a dogwood bark
if a dogwood's bark could "BARK"?
Would a dogwood bark
one billion barks in a Whistler park
from dawn to dark?
Or would a dogwood never bark
even for a dogwood lark?

The Pacific dogwood is the provincial flower of British Columbia.

Peter Pitcher Planter

The pitcher plant is the provincial flower of Newfoundland.

Peter Pitcher Planter
planted pitcher plants,
planted in his socks
and his purple underpants,
planted Parson's Pond
all the way to Witless Bay,
then Peter Pitcher Planter
threw his underwear away.
How many plants did he plant in a day?

Canada Can Cancan

Canada can boogie
in a frying pan.
But when can it do
the Canada cancan?
Canada can hip hop
in a frozen van.
But when can it do
the Canada cancan?
Canada can breakdance
on a sugar flan.
But when can it do
the Canada cancan?
Oh, Canada can cancan,
cancan high —
when the maple leaf's in the sky,
on Canada day, the first of July,
Canada cancans, kicking high.
Come, cancan Canada,
cancan with me,
and wave a maple leaf from
sea to sea to sea.

No Common Tune

Loon wrote a tune
and sang it to Bear.
Bear hibernated.
Loon sang it to Hare.
Hare hopped away.
Loon sang it to Moose.
Moose yawned and burped.
Loon sang it to Goose.
Goose laid an egg.
Loon sang it to Skunk.
Skunk sprayed stink
until Loon stunk.
“They’re all too common
for my tune.
So I’ll sing,” said Loon,
“to the full bright moon.”

The common loon is the provincial bird of Ontario.

The Rocket

You'll be an actor,
You, a baseball star,
You, a rock singer
with a mean guitar.
You'll be Prime Minister
with money in your pocket,
and you'll play hockey
just like The Rocket!

Calgary Crow

Calgary Crow,
Bow-skating guy,
laces his skates,
says, "I'm ready to fly!
a triple lutz,
a double salchow,
a bunny hop,
then I'll take a bow.
I'll crow with pride
as I fly the Bow.
Skating's a breeze
for this
Calgary crow!"

Winnipeg Mosquitoes

When Winnipeg mosquitoes
come at 8,
Winnipeg mosquitoes
make a date.
When Winnipeg mosquitoes
come at 9,
Winnipeg mosquitoes
are ready to dine!
When Winnipeg mosquitoes
come at 10,
Say your prayers
'cause it's AMEN!
When Winnipeg mosquitoes
come at 11,
They carry you off
to Mosquito Heaven.

Coppermine Caribou

Coppermine caribou
wait for Halloween.
They hide in mines
where they're not seen.
Then Coppermine caribou
creep up to you
and in a herd
give a car - i -
BOOOOOOOOOOOOOO!

Great Grey Owl

A great grey owl
rode a Red River cart
through pea-green grass
with her blue sweetheart.
She took a peach dog
and a chestnut cat.
She had on her head
an eggshell hat.
She wore lemon shoes
and aubergine socks,
and bumped over orange
and tangerine rocks.
With a skittle and a skaddle
the cart fell apart,
and off flew the owl
with her blue sweetheart!

The great grey owl is the provincial bird of Manitoba.

Bear Style

"Black's my colour,"
Polar Bear sighed.
"White's my style!"
Brown Bear cried.
Black Bear moaned:
"And brown suits me!"
So they all changed coats
beary merrily
And went on their way
beary happily!

Go A-Fishin'

"Oh, find me a dory
with a piddle paddle oary
And find me a hook
with a hiddle haddle look
And find me some bait
with a biddle baddle mate
And we'll go a-fishin'
with a widdle waddle wishin'
On a diddle daddle day!"
said Daddy Osprey.

The osprey is the provincial bird of Nova Scotia.

Wheat-Pool Weather

It's wheat-pool weather
        on the prairies today
so throw off your clothes
        and hurry away!

Manitoba's wheat pools,
Alberta's too,
Saskatchewan's wheat pools
are waiting for you.

Wheat-pool weather is hot and dry
under a pool-blue summer sky.
Wheat-pool weather can crack and fry
eggs on the sidewalk, if you try.

So rush to a wheat pool
        (forget those clothes)
Spray up the wheat
        with your fingers and toes.
Splash and frolic
        and greet the heat:
Let the grains rain
        down to your feet.

Rush to a wheat pool,
bike, hike, fly
under this summer
wheat-pool sky.

It may not last
another day
so toss off your clothes
and hurry to play.

Manitoba's wheat pools,
Alberta's too,
Saskatchewan's wheat pools
are waiting for you!

A Safe Harbour

Lighthouse
by the evening sea,
light a safe sleep harbour for me.
Night-light my house,
my room,
my bed.
Blink bright dreams
into my head.
Warn dark stormy dreams away,
Keep me safe,
come what may.
Then …
wink me awake
and nudge me to day,
light up the shores
where I like to play.

I Sleep

Rivers run
lakes lap
oceans wave
I nap

Cedars sway
willows weep
maples stir
I sleep

Moon streams
lights beam
stars shine
I dream

Index of Poem Titles

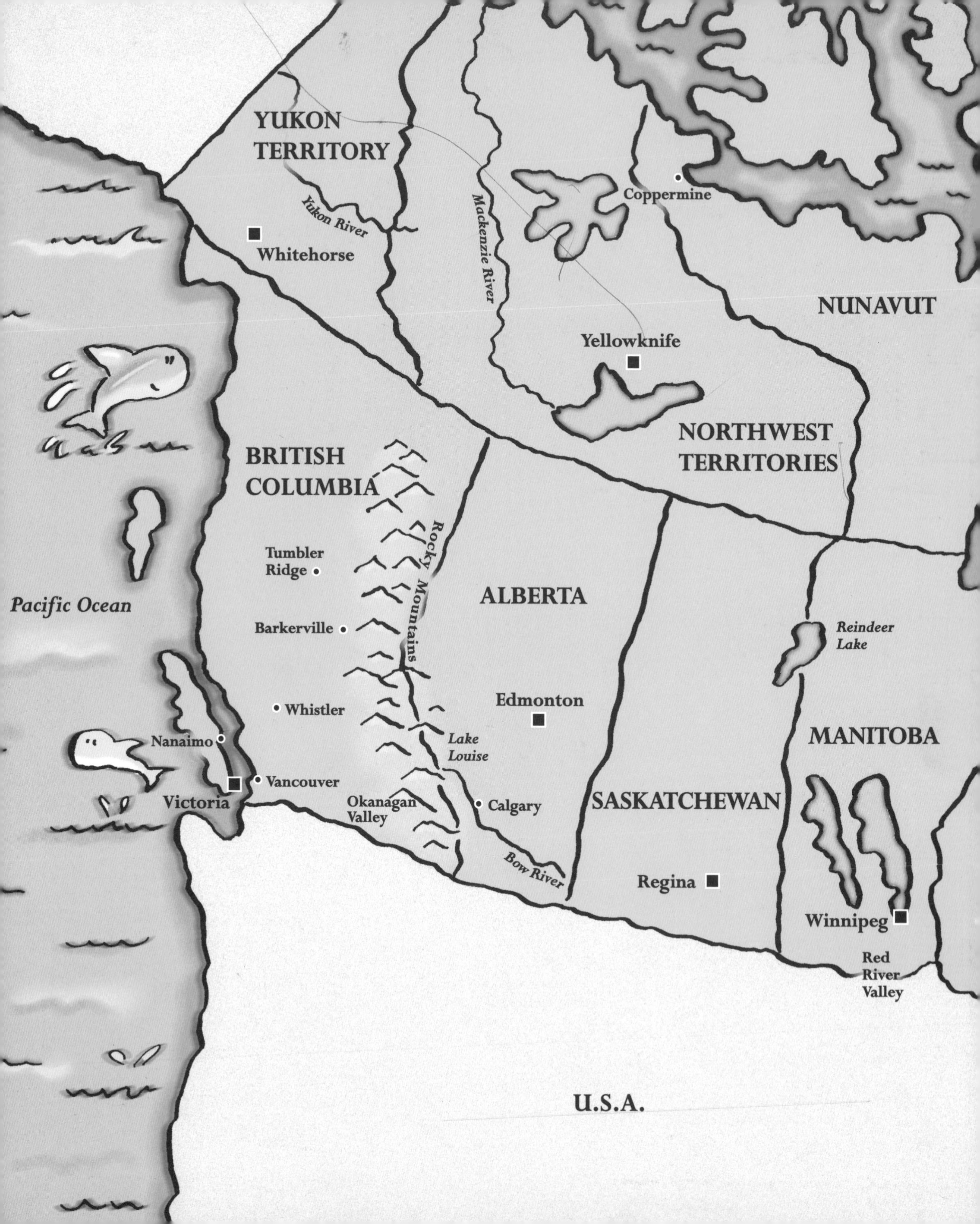
YUKON TERRITORY
Yukon River
Whitehorse
Mackenzie River
Coppermine
NUNAVUT
Yellowknife
NORTHWEST TERRITORIES
BRITISH COLUMBIA
Rocky Mountains
Tumbler Ridge
ALBERTA
Pacific Ocean
Barkerville
Reindeer Lake
Whistler
Edmonton
MANITOBA
Nanaimo
Lake Louise
Vancouver
Victoria
Okanagan Valley
Calgary
SASKATCHEWAN
Bow River
Regina
Winnipeg
Red River Valley
U.S.A.